WHO HQ
AF386782

To Karen and David Luchini, who always
let me write (and play One Direction
loudly in the house)—OL

To Ricky, who lights up my world
like nobody else—YM

PENGUIN WORKSHOP
An imprint of Penguin Random House LLC
1745 Broadway, New York, NY 10019
penguinrandomhouse.com

Copyright © 2026 by Penguin Random House LLC

Penguin Random House values and supports copyright. Copyright fuels creativity,
encourages diverse voices, promotes free speech, and creates a vibrant culture. Thank you for
buying an authorized edition of this book and for complying with copyright laws by not
reproducing, scanning, or distributing any part of it in any form without permission. You are
supporting writers and allowing Penguin Random House to continue to publish books for
every reader. Please note that no part of this book may be used or reproduced in any
manner for the purpose of training artificial intelligence technologies or systems.

PENGUIN is a registered trademark and PENGUIN WORKSHOP is a trademark of Penguin Books Ltd.
WHO HQ & Design is a registered trademark of Penguin Random House LLC.

Design by Taylor Abatiell
Text set in Adobe Garamond Pro

The art was created using a gouache brush in Adobe Photoshop.

Library of Congress Cataloging-in-Publication Data is available.

First published in the United States of America by Penguin Workshop, 2026

Manufactured in China
HH

ISBN 9798217144198
10 9 8 7 6 5 4 3 2 1

The authorized representative in the EU for product safety and compliance is Penguin Random House Ireland,
Morrison Chambers, 32 Nassau Street, Dublin D02 YH68, Ireland, https://eu-contact.penguin.ie.

HARRY STYLES

A WHO HQ ILLUSTRATED BIOGRAPHY

by
Olivia Luchini

illustrated by
Yenna Mariana

PENGUIN WORKSHOP

Dressed in their fanciest outfits, famous singers and celebrities gathered in Los Angeles on February 5, 2023, for the 65th Annual Grammy Awards. The award show honored all the best music that had been released over the past year, and everyone was eager to find out who won the biggest awards. One of those awards was Album of the Year.

At the end of the night, the microphone was handed over to an excited fan who got to announce the winner. A young pop star in a white jacket went to accept the award.

WHO WAS THAT YEAR'S BIG WINNER?

On February 1, 1994, Harry Styles was welcomed into the world by his parents, Anne Twist and Desmond Styles. He had one older sister named Gemma. Harry was born in Redditch, Worcestershire, which is a town in England. Soon after Harry was born, he and his family moved to Holmes Chapel, Cheshire, England. This is where Harry grew up.

When Harry was a little boy, he loved to listen to music in the car with his parents and sing along. Eventually, his grandfather gifted him his very own karaoke machine so that Harry could practice singing his favorite songs. One of Harry's favorite singers was Elvis Presley.

When Harry was fourteen, he began working at a local bakery. There, he sold loaves of bread, cakes, and other baked goods to customers. Like many teenagers, Harry was simply doing this job to make a little extra money. His true dream job was to be a singer, so he started working hard to make that dream reality.

He created a band with several of his friends, and they soon discovered that they were quite good together. They even won a Battle of the Bands competition! During their performance, Harry felt a rush of emotions. He loved being in front of a crowd and entertaining them.

Harry's mother was very supportive of his dream to be a professional singer. When she heard that a popular singing-competition show called *The X-Factor* was holding auditions in 2010, she signed Harry up. He was just sixteen years old!

Though Harry loved to perform, he was nervous about auditioning. What if he wasn't good enough? During his first audition, he didn't perform his song very well because he was overwhelmed. The judges asked if he could sing another song. Harry decided to sing "Isn't She Lovely" by Stevie Wonder. The judges were impressed.

Harry made it to the next round, but he wasn't selected to move on to the live shows that would be shown on TV. He was absolutely crushed. The young singer was crying in the hallway, but then a crew member from the show came out and asked Harry to come with him.

To Harry's surprise, the judges had decided to put him in a group with four other singers. Their names were Niall Horan, Liam Payne, Zayn Malik, and Louis Tomlinson. The boys would get to stay on the show, but they'd compete together. Though they had never met before *The X-Factor*, the five singers became fast friends.

The five members settled on a name for their group: One Direction. Harry had suggested the name just a few weeks before their first live performance, and all the boys thought it was great. One Direction placed third on *The X-Factor*, but they were quickly becoming very popular. People from all over the world were obsessed with the young singers.

Though they hadn't won the competition, they had still done well enough to earn a recording contract. In 2011, they released their first song. It was called "What Makes You Beautiful" and it became an instant hit. The boys were suddenly being asked to perform all over the world, and thousands of fans were showing up to cheer for them.

From 2011 to 2015, the band traveled all over the world and performed in sold-out stadiums. They released five albums and went on four massive tours. A documentary movie was even released to show fans (who called themselves "Directioners") a behind-the-scenes look at life on the road between concerts.

After Zayn abruptly left the group in March, the four remaining members of One Direction released their fifth album, *Made in the A.M.*, at the end of 2015. With no plans to tour and rumors of a breakup swirling, they officially parted ways in January 2016 after six busy years. The boys wanted to go on their own adventures and produce their own music. Harry got to thinking about what kind of songs he wanted to create.

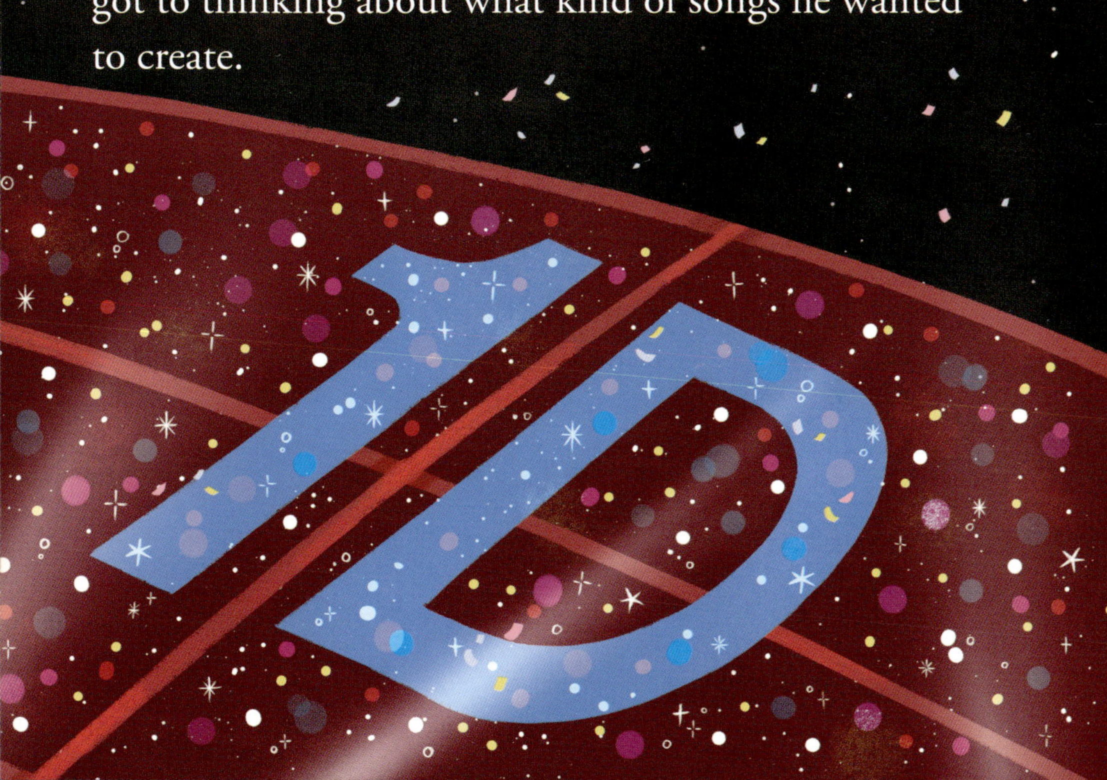

Harry put together a new backing band and then traveled with them to Jamaica. The group of musicians stayed in a house on the beautiful tropical island. There, they began writing Harry's very first solo album. It sounded very different from anything One Direction had made, and Harry adored being creative in the studio.

On May 12, 2017, Harry released the album. Its title was simply *Harry Styles*. Two of the most popular songs from the album were "Sign of the Times" and "Two Ghosts." After the album was released, Harry went on tour to share his new music. He was nervous to take the stage on his own, but he deeply missed performing and was happy to be in front of a crowd once more.

While Harry was still on tour playing music from his first album, he began recording his second album. Harry felt that the new songs he was writing were even more fun than the songs he had written for *Harry Styles*, and he was excited to release them into the world. When the tour for his first album ended, Harry lived in Japan for a little while and focused on perfecting his next songs.

On December 13, 2019, Harry released *Fine Line.* Fans immediately fell in love with the new music, especially songs such as "Treat People with Kindness" and "Adore You." He received his first ever Grammy Award for a song on the album called "Watermelon Sugar."

HARRY IN HOLLYWOOD

Before Harry released his first solo album, he tried acting in a movie for the first time. He was cast in famous director Christopher Nolan's 2017 movie *Dunkirk*, which was about soldiers during World War II. Moviegoers thought that Harry did an amazing job in his first movie. He loved being on a film set and decided to pursue more acting roles in Hollywood.

In 2021, Harry joined the Marvel Cinematic Universe when he played Eros, the god of love, in *Eternals*. Directors have continued to cast Harry in their films, and Harry has continued to enjoy acting alongside making music.

The tour for *Fine Line* was supposed to begin in April 2020, but then the COVID-19 pandemic began. Because of this, Harry's concerts were all postponed until it was safer for people to be close together again. For the first time in years, Harry was forced to slow down and stay put.

Soon after the pandemic started, Harry found the inspiration to make music again. He began getting to work on his third album and poured his heart into new song lyrics that felt more personal than ever. When it was safe, he got his band together and began recording the songs in a nearby studio.

On May 20, 2022, *Harry's House* was released. Since enough time had passed since the beginning of the pandemic, Harry was able to perform a massive concert in New York the same day that his album came out. The show was called "One Night Only in New York."

When the curtain dropped and the music began playing, Harry burst into action. He danced across the stage and sang at the top of his lungs. The crowd had already memorized the lyrics to the songs that had just come out that day. It was a special night for a special album.

After "One Night Only in New York," Harry began performing the songs from *Harry's House* on a worldwide tour. Fans fell in love with the new songs, especially "As It Was" and "Matilda." They created fun outfits to wear to Harry's shows that were bold and colorful, just like the costumes Harry wore.

Harry's House went on to win many awards, and Harry was very proud of creating such a successful album. But one of the things he was proudest of was how his music made listeners feel. Harry's concerts were places where people felt like they could be their most authentic selves and be accepted for who they were, and that made Harry very happy.

HARRY'S AWARD SHELF

As a solo artist, Harry has received over 300 award nominations during his career, and he has won over 130 of those. Here are just a few of his wins!

- Three Grammy Awards
- Six Brit Awards
- Three American Music Awards
- Four MTV Video Music Awards
- One Billboard Music Award

When he was a member of One Direction, the band also won several awards, including the following:

- Six Billboard Music Awards
- Seven Brit Awards
- Seven American Music Awards
- Twenty-Eight Teen Choice Awards

That's a lot of trophies!

Over the course of his career, Harry has released over 120 songs and performed over 500 concerts for his excited fans. He has performed with legendary musicians, like Stevie Nicks and Shania Twain. He's come a long way from singing their songs in the car as a little boy!

Not too long ago, Harry was a teenager who was left brokenhearted after being cut from a singing competition. But he has kept performing, creating, and dreaming. There is no telling what amazing things this icon will do next.

BIBLIOGRAPHY

***Books for young readers**

*Anderson, Kirsten. *Who Is Harry Styles?* New York: Penguin
   Workshop, 2023.

"Artist: Harry Styles." Grammy Awards. https://www.grammy.com/
   artists/harry-styles/287522.

"Harry Styles." *Britannica Kids*. https://kids.britannica.com/
   students/article/Harry-Styles/635493.

Rogers, Kara. "Harry Styles." *Britannica*. Updated March 2025.
   https://www.britannica.com/biography/Harry-Styles.

Spanos, Brittany. "Harry's House: How Harry Styles Became the
   World's Most Wanted Man." *Rolling Stone*. August 22, 2022.
   https://www.rollingstone.com/music/music-features/harry-
   styles-harrys-house-dont-worry-darling-my-policeman-
   cover-1397290/.

TIMELINE

1994 — Harry Styles is born in Redditch, Worcestershire, England

2010 — Auditions for *The X-Factor*

2011 — One Direction releases their first album, *Up All Night*

2012 — One Direction releases their second album, *Take Me Home*

2013 — One Direction releases their third album, *Midnight Memories*

One Direction releases their fourth album, *Four*	**2014**
One Direction releases their final album, *Made in the A.M.*	**2015**
Dunkirk releases in theaters	**2017**
Releases his first solo album, *Harry Styles*	
Releases *Fine Line*	**2019**
Eternals releases in theaters	**2021**
Releases *Harry's House*	**2022**
Wins the Grammy for Album of the Year	**2023**